MOST OF THE DOCUMENTED COMMANDMENTS OF JESUS CHRIST

Also by Rolland E. Stroup, Jr.

A TREASURY OF HEAVEN'S LIKENESSES

WASHINGTON'S WIT MODERNLY WRIT with
SOLOMON'S NEW LEAF and
THOUGHTS FROM THE EARLY 21ST CENTURY

DISTILLED LINCOLN ANECDOTES

LATTER-DAY RICHARD

MOST OF THE DOCUMENTED COMMANDMENTS OF JESUS CHRIST

Source of bible verses: **Holy Bible**
World English Bible Version
A public domain work published by
Bible Domain Publishing 2016

Words of Jesus Christ as presented in the Book of John, Chapter 14, Verse 21: One who has my commandments and keeps them, that person is one who loves me. One who loves me will be loved by my Father, and I will love him, and will reveal myself to him.

ROLLAND E. STROUP, JR

MOST OF THE DOCUMENTED COMMANDMENTS OF JESUS CHRIST

iUniverse books may be ordered through booksellers or by contacting:

iUniverse
1663 Liberty Drive
Bloomington, IN 47403
www.iuniverse.com
844-349-9409

Because of the dynamic nature of the Internet, any web addresses or links contained in this book may have changed since publication and may no longer be valid. The views expressed in this work are solely those of the author and do not necessarily reflect the views of the publisher, and the publisher hereby disclaims any responsibility for them.

Any people depicted in stock imagery provided by Getty Images are models, and such images are being used for illustrative purposes only. Certain stock imagery © Getty Images.

ISBN: 978-1-6632-3176-5 (sc)
ISBN: 978-1-6632-3177-2 (e)

Print information available on the last page.

iUniverse rev. date: 12/08/2021

LIST OF TOPICS OF THE COMMANDMENTS DEVELOPED BY ROLLAND E. STROUP, JR.

TOPICS WITH RELATED COMMANDMENTS PRESENTED IN ALPHABETICAL ORDER BY ROLLAND E. STROUP, JR.

Notes to the reader:

Many of the verses or series of verses of the source Holy Bible are repeated here under more than one topic because they are so related.

Some of the beginning and ending quotation marks of sentences here quoted may appear to be missing due to limits on the length of the quotations.

Some verses or portions of verses in passages quoted from the source Holy Bible are omitted here, as shown by ellipses; therefore, quotations taken from this book should not be solely attributed to the source Holy Bible.

Adultery

Matthew 5, 27 "You have heard that it was said, 'You shall not commit adultery;' 28 but I tell you that everyone who gazes at a woman to lust after her has committed adultery with her already in his heart."

Luke 16, 18 Everyone who divorces his wife and marries another commits adultery. He who marries one who is divorced from a husband commits adultery.

Asking for, Seeking for, Knocking

Luke 11, 9 "I tell you, keep asking, and it will be given you. Keep seeking, and you will find. Keep knocking, and it will be opened to you. 10 For everyone who asks receives. He who seeks finds. To him who knocks it will be opened."

John 16, 24 Until now, you have asked nothing in my name. Ask, and you will receive, that your joy may be made full.

Attitude during Adversity

Matthew 5, 11 "Blessed are you when people reproach you, persecute you, and say all kinds of evil against you falsely, for my sake. 12 Rejoice, and be exceedingly glad, for great is your reward in heaven. For that is how they persecuted the prophets who were before you."

Luke 6,22 "Blessed are you when men hate you, and when they exclude and mock you, and throw out your name as evil, for the Son of Man's sake. 23 Rejoice in that day, and leap for joy, for behold, your reward is great in heaven, for their fathers did the same thing to the prophets."

Luke 12, 58 For when you are going with your adversary before the magistrate, try diligently on the way to be released from him, lest perhaps he drag you to the judge, and the judge deliver you to the officer, and the officer throw you into prison.

Avoiding Court Trial

Matthew 5,25 "Agree with your adversary quickly, while you are with him on way; lest perhaps the prosecutor deliver you to the judge, and the judge deliver you to the officer, and you be cast into prison."

Luke 12,58 "For when you are going with your adversary before the magistrate, try diligently on the way to be released from him, lest perhaps he drag you to the judge, and the judge deliver you to the officer, and the officer throw you into prison."

Avoiding Scandals

Luke 17,1 He said to the disciples, "It is impossible that no occasions of stumbling should come, but woe to him through whom they come! 2 It would be better for him if a millstone were hung around his neck, and he were thrown into the sea, rather than that he should cause one of these little ones to stumble."

Baptism of Jesus

Matthew 3, 13 Then Jesus came from Galilee to the Jordan to John, to be baptized by him. 14 But John would have hindered him, saying, "I need to be baptized by you, and you come to me?" 15 But Jesus, answering, said to him, "Allow it now, for this is the fitting way for us to fulfill all righteousness."

Behave like Christ and do his deeds

John 13,14 "For I have given you an example, that you should also do as I have done to you."

Believe in Jesus

Mark 16, 16 He who believes and is baptized will be saved; but he who disbelieves will be condemned.

John 6, 40 This is the will of the one who sent me, that everyone who sees the Son, and believes in him, should have eternal life; and I will raise him up at the last day."

John 10, 37 If I don't do the works of my Father, don't believe me. 38 But if I do them, though you don't believe me, believe the works, that you may know and believe that the Father is in me, and I in the Father."

John 14, 11 Believe me that I am in the Father, and the Father in me; or else believe me for the very works' sake.

John 20, 27 Then he said to Thomas, "Reach here your finger, and see my hands. Reach here your hand, and put it into my side. Don't be unbelieving, but believing."

Be One with Jesus

John 15, 4 Remain in me, and I in you. As the branch can't bear fruit by itself unless it remains in the vine, so neither can you, unless you remain in me.

Blessing

Luke 6, 28 ". . . bless those who curse you, and pray for those who mistreat you."

Calamities

Matthew 24, 4 Jesus answered them, "Be careful that no one leads you astray. 5 For many will come in my name, saying, 'I am the Christ,' and will lead many astray. 6 You will hear of wars and rumors of war. See that you aren't troubled, for all this must happen, but the end is not yet."

Matthew 24,15 "When, therefore, you see the abomination of desolation, which was spoken of through Daniel the prophet, standing in the holy place (let the reader understand), 16 then let those who are in Judea flee to the mountains. 17 Let him who is on the housetop not go down to take out the things that are in his house. 18 Let him who is in the field not return back to get his clothes. . . . 20 Pray that your flight will not be in winter, nor on a Sabbath, 21 for then there will be great suffering, such as has not been since the beginning of the world until now, no, nor ever will be. 22 Unless those days had been shortened, no flesh would have been saved. 23 Then if any man tells you, 'Behold, here is the Christ,' or, 'There,' don't believe it."

Matthew 24, 42 "Watch therefore, for you don't know in what hour your Lord comes." 44 Therefore also be ready, for in an hour that you don't expect, the Son of Man will come.

Matthew 25,13 "Watch therefore, for you don't know the day nor the hour in which the Son of Man is coming."

Mark 13, 5 Jesus, answering, began to tell them, "Be careful that no one leads you astray. 6 For many will come in my name, saying, 'I am he!' and will lead many astray. 7 "When you hear of wars and rumors of wars, don't be troubled. For those must happen, but the end is not yet.... 9 But watch yourselves, for they will deliver you up to councils. You will be beaten in synagogues. You will stand before rulers and kings for my sake, for a testimony to them. . . . 14 But when you see the abomination of desolation, spoken by Daniel the prophet, standing where it ought not" (let the reader understand), "then let those who are in Judea flee to the mountains, 15 and let him who is on the housetop not go down, nor enter in, to take anything out of his house. 16 Let him who is in the field not return back to take his cloak…. 18 Pray that your flight won't be in winter. 19 For in those days there will be oppression, such as there has not been the like from the beginning of the creation which God created until now, and never will be. 20 Unless the Lord had shortened the days, no flesh would have been saved; but for the sake of the chosen ones, whom he picked out, he shortened the days. 21 Then if anyone tells you, 'Look, here is the Christ!' or, 'Look, there!' don't believe it. 22 For there will arise false christs and false prophets, and will show signs and wonders, that they may lead astray, if possible, even the chosen ones. 23 But you watch. . . . 28 "Now from the fig tree learn this parable. When the branch has now become tender, and produces its leaves, you know that the summer is near; 29 even so you also, when you see these things coming to pass, know that it is near, at the doors. . . . 33 Watch, keep alert, and pray; for you don't know when the time is. . . . 37 What I tell you, I tell all: watch."

Luke 12, 40 Therefore be ready also, for the Son of Man is coming in an hour that you don't expect him."

Luke 17, 31 In that day he who will be on the housetop and his goods in the house, let him not go down to take them away. Let him who is in the field likewise not turn back. 32 Remember Lot's wife!

Luke 21, 8 He said, "Watch out that you don't get led astray, for many will come in my name, saying, 'I am he,' and, 'The time is at hand.' Therefore don't follow them. . . . 20 "But when you see Jerusalem surrounded by armies, then know that its desolation is at hand. . . . 28 But when these things begin to happen, look up and lift up your heads, because your redemption is near.". . . 31 Even so you also, when you see these things happening, know that God's Kingdom is near. . . . 34 "So be careful, or your hearts will be loaded down with carousing, drunkenness, and cares of this life, and that day will come on you suddenly. . . . 36 Therefore be watchful all the time, praying that you may be counted worthy to escape all these things that will happen, and to stand before the Son of Man."

Children

Matthew 18, 2 Jesus called a little child to himself, and set him in the middle of them, 3 and said, "Most certainly I tell you, unless you turn, and become as little children, you in no way enter into the Kingdom of Heaven."

Matthew 18,10 "See that you don't despise one of these little ones, for I tell you that in heaven their angels always see the face of my Father who is in heaven."

Matthew 19,14 But Jesus said, "Allow the little children, and don't forbid them to come to me; for the Kingdom of Heaven belongs to ones like these."

Mark 9, 42 Whoever will cause one of these little ones who believe in me to stumble, it would be better for him if he were thrown into the sea with a millstone hung around his neck.

Mark 10, 14 . . . "Allow the little children to come to me! Don't forbid them, for God's kingdom belongs to such as these. 15 "Most certainly I tell you, whoever will not receive God's Kingdom like a little child, he will in no way enter into it."

Luke 17, 1 He said to his disciples, "It is impossible that no occasions of stumbling should come, but woe to him through whom they come! 2 It would be better for him if a millstone were hung around his neck, and he were thrown into the sea, rather than that he should cause one of these little ones to stumble."

Luke 18, 16 "Allow the little children to come to me, and don't hinder them, for God's kingdom belongs to such as these. 17 Most certainly, I tell you, whoever doesn't receive God's kingdom like a little child, he will in no way enter into it."

Christ's Mission

Matthew 5, 17 "Don't think that I came to destroy the law or the prophets. I didn't come to destroy, but to fulfill.

Commandments to Follow to Receive Eternal Life

Matthew 19, 16 Behold, one came to him and said, "Good teacher, what good things shall I do that I may have eternal life?" 17 He said to him, "Why do you call me good? No one is good but one, that is, God. But if you want to enter into life, keep the commandments." 18 He said to him, "Which ones?" Jesus said, "'You shall not murder.' 'You shall not commit adultery.' 'You shall not steal.' 'You shall not offer false testimony.' 19 'Honor your father and your mother.' And, 'You shall love your neighbor as yourself.'"

Mark 10, 17 As he was going out into the way, one ran to him, knelt before him, and asked him, "Good Teacher, what shall I do that I might inherit eternal life?" Jesus said to him, "Why do you call me good? No one is good except one—God. 19 You know the commandments: 'Do not murder,' 'Do not commit adultery,' 'Do not steal,' 'Do not give false testimony,' 'Do not defraud,' 'Honor your father and mother.'"

Luke 13, 23 One said to him, "Lord, are they few who are saved?" He said to them, 24 "Strive to enter in by the narrow door, for many, I tell you, will seek to enter in and will not be able.

Luke 18, 18 A certain ruler asked him, saying, "Good Teacher, what shall I do to to inherit eternal life? 19 Jesus asked him, "Why do you call me good? No one is good, except one: God. 20 You know the commandments: 'Don't commit adultery,' 'Don't murder,' 'Don't steal,' 'Don't give false testimony,' 'Honor your father and your mother.'"

John 6, 40 This is the will of the one who sent me, that everyone who sees the Son, and believes in him, should have eternal life; and I will raise him up on the last day."

John 6, 53 Jesus therefore said to them, "Most certainly I tell you, unless you eat the flesh of the Son of Man and drink his blood, you don't have life in yourselves. 54 He who eats my flesh and drinks my blood has eternal life, and I will raise him up on the last day. 55 For my flesh is food indeed, and my blood is drink indeed. 56 He who eats my flesh and drinks my blood lives in me, and I in him. 57 As the living Father sent me, and I live because of the Father; so he who feeds on me, he will also live because of me. 58 This is the bread which came down out of heaven—not as our fathers ate the manna, and died. He who eats this bread will live forever."

Commandments in Addition to the ones above for the Rich to Receive Eternal Life after Asking Jesus about it

Matthew 19, 20 The young man said to him, "All these things I have observed from my youth. What do I still lack?" 21 Jesus said to him, "If you want to be perfect, go, sell what you have, and give to the poor, and you will have treasure in heaven; and come, follow me." 22 But when the young man heard the saying, he went away sad, for he was one who had great possessions.

Mark 10, 20 He said to him, "Teacher, I have observed these things from my youth." 21 Jesus looking at him loved him, and said to him, "One thing you lack. Go, sell whatever you have, and give to the poor, and you will have treasure in heaven; and come, follow me, taking up the cross." 22 But his face fell at that saying, and he went away sorrowful, for he was one who had great possessions.

Luke 18, 21 He said, "I have observed all these things from my youth up." 22 When Jesus heard these things, he said to him, "You still lack one thing. Sell all that you have and distribute it to the poor. Then you will have treasure in heaven;

then come, follow me." 23 But when he heard these things, he became very sad, for he was very rich.

Commandments to the Twelve Apostles for their Travels to Announce the Arrival of the Kingdom of Heaven

Matthew 10, 5 Jesus sent these twelve out, and commanded them, saying, "Don't go among the Gentiles, and don't enter into any city of the Samaritans. 6 Rather, go to the lost sheep of the house of Israel. 7 As you go, preach, saying, 'The Kingdom of Heaven is at hand!" 8 Heal the sick, cleanse the lepers, and cast out demons. Freely you received, so freely give. 9 Don't take any gold, silver, or brass in your money belts. 10 Take no bag for your journey, neither two coats, nor shoes, nor staff: for the laborer is worthy of his food. 11 Into whatever city or village you enter, find out who in it is worthy; and stay there until you go on. 12 As you enter into the household, greet it. 13 If the household is worthy, let your peace come on it, but if it isn't worthy, let your peace return to you. 14 Whoever doesn't receive you, nor hear your words, as you go out of that house or that city, shake the dust off your feet. . . . 16 "Behold, I send you out as sheep among wolves. Therefore be wise as serpents, and harmless as doves. 17 But beware of men: for they will deliver you up to councils and in their synagogues they will scourge you. . . . 23 But when they persecute you in this city, flee into the next, . . .

Condemning

Matthew 21, 18 Now in the morning, as he returned to the city, he was hungry. 19 Seeing a fig tree by the road, he came to it and found nothing on it but leaves. He said to it, "Let there be no fruit from you forever!" Immediately the fig tree withered away.

Luke 6, 37 Don't judge and you won't be judged. Don't condemn and you won't be condemned. Set free, and you will be set free.

Divorce

Matthew 19, 9 I tell you that whoever divorces his wife, except for sexual immorality, and marries another, commits adultery; and he who marries her when she is divorced commits adultery."

Mark 10, 9 What therefore God has joined together, let no man separate."

Mark 10, 11 He said to them, "Whoever divorces his wife, and marries another, commits adultery against her. 12 If a woman herself divorces her husband, and marries another, she commits adultery."

Luke 16,18 Everyone who divorces his wife and marries another commits adultery. He who marries one who is divorced from a husband commits adultery.

Doing Good

Luke 6, 27 "But I tell you who hear: love your enemies, do good to those who hate you,

Luke 6, 35 But love your enemies, and do good, . . .

Entrance into Jerusalem

Matthew 21, . . . 2 saying to them, "Go into the village that is opposite you, and immediately you will find a donkey tied, and a colt with her. Untie them, and bring them to me. 3 If anyone says anything to you, you shall say, 'The Lord needs them,' and immediately he will send them."

Faith and Healing

Matthew 8, 8 The centurion answered, "Lord, I am not worthy for you to come under my roof. Just say the word, and my servant will be healed. . . . 13 Jesus said to the centurion, "Go your way. Let it be done for you as you have believed."

Matthew 9, 2 Behold, they brought to him a man who was paralyzed, lying on a bed. Jesus, seeing their faith, said to the paralytic, "Son, cheer up! Your sins are forgiven you." . . . . 6 . . . . "Get up, and take up your mat, and go to your house. 7 He arose and departed to his house.

Matthew 9, 27 As Jesus passed by from there, two blind men followed him, calling out and saying, "Have mercy on us, son of David!" 28 When he had come into the house, the blind men came to him. Jesus said to them, "Do you believe that I am able to do this?" They told him, "Yes, Lord." 29 Then he touched their eyes, saying, "According to your faith be it done to you." 30 Their eyes were opened.

Matthew 10, 1 He called to himself his twelve disciples, and gave them authority over unclean spirits, to cast them out, and to heal every disease and every sickness.

Mark 5, 34 He said to her, "Daughter, your faith has made you well. Go in peace, and be cured of your disease."

Mark 10, 51 Jesus asked him, "What do you want me to do for you?" The blind man said to him, "Rabboni, that I may see again." 52 Jesus said to him, "Go your way. Your faith has made you well." Immediately he received his sight, and followed Jesus on the way.

Luke 8, 48 He said to her, "Daughter, cheer up. Your faith has made you well. Go in peace." 49 While he still spoke, one from the ruler of the synagogue's house came, saying to him, "Your daughter is dead. Don't trouble the Teacher." 50 But Jesus hearing it, answered him, "Don't be afraid. Only believe, and she will be healed."

Luke 17,12 As he entered into a certain village, ten men who were lepers met him, who stood at a distance. 13 They lifted up their voices saying, "Jesus, Master, have mercy on us!" 14 When he saw them, he said to them, "Go show yourselves to the priests." As they went, they were cleansed. 15 One of them, when he saw that he was healed, turned back, glorifying God with a loud voice. 16 He fell on his face at Jesus' feet, giving him thanks; and he was a Samaritan. 17 Jesus answered, "Weren't the ten cleansed? But where are the nine? 18 Were there none found who returned to give glory to God, except this foreigner?" 19 Then he said to him, "Get up, and go your way. Your faith has healed you."

Luke 18, 35 As he came near Jericho, a certain blind man sat by the road, begging. 36 Hearing a multitude going by, he asked what this meant. 37 They told him that Jesus of Nazareth was passing by. 38 He cried out, "Jesus, you son of David, have mercy on me!" 39 Those who led the way rebuked him, that he should be quiet; but he cried out all the more, "You son of David, have mercy on me!" 40 Standing still, Jesus commanded him to be brought to him. When he had come near, he asked him, 41 "What do you want me to do?" He said, "Lord, that I may see again." 42 Jesus said to him. "Receive your sight. Your faith has healed you." 43 Immediately he received his sight and followed him, glorifying God. All the people, when they saw it, praised God.

John 4, 46 Jesus therefore again came to Cana of Galilee, where he had made the water into wine. There was a certain nobleman whose son was sick at Capernaum. 47 When he heard that Jesus had come out of Judea into Galilee, he went to him and begged him that he would come down and heal his son, for he was at the point of death. 48 Jesus therefore said to him, "Unless you see signs and wonders, you will in no way believe." 49 The nobleman said to him, "Sir, come down before my child dies." 50 Jesus said to him, "Go your way. Your son lives." The man believed the word that Jesus spoke to him, and he went his way. 51 As he was now going down, his servants met him and reported, saying "Your child lives!" 52 So he inquired of them the hour when he began to get better. They said therefore to him, "Yesterday at the seventh hour, the fever left him." 53 So the father knew that it was at that hour in which Jesus said to him, "Your son lives." He believed, as did his whole house.

John 5, 5 A certain man was there who had been sick for thirty-eight years. 6 When Jesus saw him lying there, and knew that he had been sick for a long time, he asked him, "Do you want to be made well?" 7 The sick man answered him, "Sir, I have no one to put me into the pool when the water is stirred up, but while I'm coming, another steps down before me." 8 Jesus said to him, "Arise, take up your mat, and walk." 9 Immediately, the man was made well, and took up his mat and walked. . . . .

John 9, 6 When he had said this, he spat on the ground, made mud with the saliva, anointed the blind man's eyes with the mud, 7 and said to him, "Go, wash in the pool of Siloam (which means "Sent"). . . . 30 The man answered them, "How amazing! You don't know where he comes from, yet he opened my eyes. 31 We know that God doesn't listen to sinners, but if anyone is a worshipper of God, and does his will, he listens to him. 32 Since the beginning of the world it has never been heard of that anyone opened the eyes of someone born blind. 33 If this man were not from God, he could do nothing." . . . 35 Jesus heard that they had thrown him out, and finding him, he said, "Do you believe in the Son of God?" 36 He answered, "Who is he, Lord, that I may believe in him?" 37 Jesus said to him, "You have both seen him, and it is he who speaks with you." 38 He said, "Lord, I believe!" and he worshipped him.

Faith and Sinning

Matthew 9, 2 Behold, they brought him a man who was paralyzed, lying on a bed. Jesus, seeing their faith, said to the paralytic, "Son, cheer up! Your sins are forgiven you." . . . 6 But that you may know that the Son of Man has authority on earth to forgive sins-" (then he said to the paralytic), "Get up, and take up you mat, and go to your house." 7 He arose and departed to his house.

John 5, 14 Afterward Jesus found him in the temple, and said to him, "Behold, you are made well. Sin no more, so that nothing worse happens to you."

John 8, 7 But when they continued asking him, he looked up and said to them, "He who is without sin among you, let him throw the first stone at her." . . . 9 They, when they heard it, being convicted by their conscience, went out one be one, beginning from the oldest, even to the last. . . .10 Jesus, standing up, saw her and said, "Woman, where are your accusers? Did no one condemn you?" 11 She said, "no one, Lord." Jesus said, "Neither do I condemn you. Go your way. From now on, sin no more."

False Prophets/Religious Frauds/False Teachings

Matthew 7, 15 "Beware of false prophets, who come to you in sheep's clothing, but inwardly are ravening wolves. 16 By their fruits you will know them.

Matthew 16, 6 Jesus said to them, "Take heed and beware of the yeast of the Pharisees and Sadducees."

Matthew 24, 4 Jesus answered them, "Be careful that no one leads you astray.

Fear/Alarm

Matthew 6, 25 Therefore I tell you; don't be anxious for your life: what you will eat, or what you will drink; nor yet your body, for what you will wear.

Matthew 10, 26 Therefore don't be afraid of them, for there is nothing covered that will not be revealed; and hidden that will not be known.

Matthew 10, 32 Therefore don't be afraid. You are of more value than many sparrows.

Matthew 14, 26 When the disciples saw him walking on the sea, they were troubled, saying, "It's a ghost!" and they cried out for fear. 27 But immediately Jesus spoke to them, saying, "Cheer up! It is I! Don't be afraid." 28 Peter answered him and said. "Lord, if it is you, command me to come to you on the waters." He said, "Come!" Peter stepped down from the boat, and walked on the waters to come to Jesus. 30 But when he saw that the wind was strong, he was afraid, and beginning to sink, he cried out, saying, "Lord, save me!" 31 Immediately Jesus stretched out his hand, took hold of him, and said to him, "You of little faith, why did you doubt?"

Matthew 17, 7 Jesus came and touched them and said, "Get up, and don't be afraid."

Matthew 24, ". . . 6 You will hear of wars and rumors of wars. See that you aren't troubled, for all this must happen, but the end is not yet.

Matthew 28, 8 They departed quickly from the tomb with fear and great joy, and ran to bring his disciples word. 9 As they went to tell his disciples, behold, Jesus met them saying, "Rejoice!" They came and took hold of his feet, and worshipped him. 10 Then Jesus said to them, "Don't be afraid. Go tell my brothers that they should go into Galilee, and there they will see me."

Mark 6, 50 for they all saw him, and were troubled. But he immediately spoke with them, and said to them, "Cheer up! It is I! Don't be afraid."

Mark 13, 7 "When you hear of wars and rumors of wars, don't be troubled. For those must happen, but the end is not yet.

Mark 13, 11 When they lead you away and deliver you up, don't be anxious beforehand, or premeditate what you will say, but say whatever will be given to you in that hour. For it is not you who speak but the Holy Spirit.

Luke 8, 49 While he still spoke, one from the ruler of the synagogue's house came, saying to him, "Your daughter is dead. Don't trouble the Teacher." 50 But Jesus hearing it, answered him, "Don't be afraid. Only believe, and she will be healed."

Luke 12, 4 "I tell you my friends, don't be afraid of those who kill the body, and after that have no more that they can do. 5 But I will tell you whom you should fear. Fear him who after he has killed, has power to cast into Gahenna. Yes, I tell you, fear him.

Luke 12, 7 But the very hairs of your head are all counted. Therefore don't be afraid.

Luke 12, 11 When they bring you before the synagogues, the rulers, and the authorities, don't be anxious how or what you will answer, or what you will say; 12 for the Holy Spirit will teach you in that same hour what you must say."

Luke 12, 22 He said to his disciples, "Therefore I tell you, don't be anxious for your life, what you will eat, nor yet for your body, what you will wear.

Luke 12, 29 Don't seek what you will eat or what you will drink; neither be anxious. 30 For the nations of the world seek after all of these things. 31 But seek God's kingdom, and all these things will be added to you. 32 Don't be afraid, little flock, for it is your Father's good pleasure to give you the Kingdom.

John 6, 18 The sea was tossed by a great wind blowing. 19 When therefore they had rowed about twenty-five or thirty stadia, they saw Jesus walking on the sea, and drawing near to the boat; and they were afraid. 20 But he said to them, "It is I. Don't be afraid."

John 20, 26 . . . . Jesus came, the doors being locked. And stood in the middle, and said, "Peace be to you."

Revelation 1, 17 When I saw him, I fell at his feet like a dead man. He laid his right hand on me, saying, "Don't be afraid.

Final Commandments to The Apostles

Matthew 28, 19 Go and make disciples of all nations, baptizing them in the name of the Father and of the Son and of the Holy Spirit, 20 teaching them to observe all things that I commanded you.

Mark 13, 10 The Good News must be preached to all nations.

Mark 16, 15 He said to them, "Go into all the world, and preach to Good News to the whole creation.

Luke 21, 14 Settle it therefore in your hearts not to meditate beforehand how to answer, 15 for I will give you a mouth and wisdom which all your adversaries will not be able to withstand or to contradict.

Luke 22, 31 The Lord said, "Simon, Simon, behold, Satan asked to have all of you, that he might sift you as wheat, 32 but I prayed for you, that your faith wouldn't fail. You, when once you have turned again, establish your brothers."

Luke 24, 49 Behold, I send out the promise of my Father on you. But wait in the city of Jerusalem until you are clothed with power from on high.

Acts 1, 4 Being assembled together with them, "Don't depart from Jerusalem, but wait for the promise of the Father, which you heard from me. 5 For John indeed baptized in water, but you will be baptized in the Holy Spirit not many days from now." . . . 8 But you will receive power when the Holy Spirit has come upon you. You will be witnesses to me in Jerusalem, in all Judea and Samaria, and to the uttermost parts of the earth."

Acts 13, 47 For so has the Lord commanded us, saying, 'I have set you as a light for the Gentiles, that you should bring salvation to the uttermost parts of the earth.'"

Fleeing

Matthew 24, 16 then let those who are in Judea flee to the mountains. Let him who is on the housetop not go down to take out things that are in his house. 18 Let him who is in the field not return back to get his clothes.

Matthew 24, 20 Pray that your flight will not be in the winter, nor on a Sabbath, 21 for then there will be great suffering, such as has not been from the beginning of the world until now, no, nor ever will be.

Mark 13, 14 But when you see the abomination of desolation, spoken of by Daniel the prophet, standing where it ought not" (let the reader understand), "then let those who are in Judea flee to the mountains, 15 and let him who is on the housetop not go down, not enter in, to take anything out of his house. 16 Let him who is in the field not return back to take his cloak.

Mark 13, 18 Pray that your flight won't be in winter. 19 For in those days there will be oppression, such as there has not been the like from the beginning of the creation which God created until now, and never will be.

Luke 17, 31 In that day, he who will be on the housetop and his goods in the house, let him not go down to take them away. Let him who is in the field likewise not turn back.

Follow Jesus

Matthew 4, 19 He said to them, "Come after me and I will make you fishers of men."

Matthew 8, 22 But Jesus said to him, "Follow me, and leave the dead to bury their own dead."

Matthew 11, 28 "Come to me, all you who labor and are heavily burdened, and I will give you rest. 29 Take my yoke upon you, and learn from me, for I am gentle and humble in heart; and you will find rest for your souls. 30 For my yoke is easy, and my burden is light."

Matthew 25, 34 Then the King will tell those on his right hand, 'Come, blessed of my Father, inherit the Kingdom prepared for you from the foundation of the world;

Mark 1, 17 Jesus said to them, "Come after me, and I will make you into fishers of men."

Luke 9, 59 He said to another, "Follow me!" But he said, "Lord, allow me first to go and bury my father." 60 But Jesus said to him, "Leave the dead to bury their own dead, but you go and announce God's Kingdom."

Follow Jesus' Commandments

Matthew 7, 13 "Enter in by the narrow gate; for wide is the gate and broad is the way that leads to destruction, and many are those who enter by it.

Matthew 7, 24 "Everyone therefore who hears these words of mine, and does them, I will liken him unto a wise man, who built his house on a rock. 25 The rain came down, the floods came, and the winds blew, and beat on that house; and it didn't fall, for it was founded on a rock.

Mark 3, 35 For whoever does the will of God is my brother, my sister, and mother."

John 6, 27 Don't work for the food which perishes, but for the food which remains to eternal life, which the Son of Man will give you. For God the Father has sealed him."

John 14, 21 One who has my commandments and keeps them, that person is one who loves me. One who loves me will be loved by my Father, and I will love him, and will reveal myself to him."

Forgiving and Pardoning

Mark 11, 25 Whenever you stand praying, forgive, if you have anything against anyone; so that your Father, who is in heaven, may also forgive your transgressions.

Luke 6, 37 Don't judge, and you won't be judged. Don't condemn, and you won't be condemned. Set free, and you will be set free.

Luke 17, 4 If he sins against you seven times in a day, and seven times returns, saying, 'I repent,' you shall forgive him."

Giving

Matthew 5, 40 If anyone sues you to take away your coat, let him have your cloak also. 41 Whoever compels you to go one mile, go with him two. 42 Give to him who asks you, and don't turn away from him who desires to borrow from you.

Matthew 6, 3 But when you do merciful deeds, don't let your left hand know what your right hand does, 4 so that your merciful deeds may be in secret, then your Father who sees in secret will reward you openly.

Matthew 25, 34 Then the King will tell those on his right hand, 'Come, blessed of my Father, inherit the Kingdom prepared for you from the foundation of the world; 35 for I was hungry, and you gave me food to eat. I was thirsty, and you gave me drink. I was a stranger, and you took me in. 36 I was naked, and you clothed me. I was sick, and you visited me. I was in prison, and you came to me.' 37 "Then the righteous will answer him, saying, 'Lord, when did we see you hungry, and feed you; or thirsty, and give you a drink? 38 When did we see you as a stranger, and take you in; or naked, and clothe you? 39 When did we see you sick, or in prison, and come to you?' 40 "The King will answer them, 'Most certainly I tell you, because you did it to one of the least of my brothers, you did it to me.'

Mark 4, 23 If any man has ears to hear, let him hear." 24 He said to them, "Take heed what you hear. With whatever measure you measure, it will be measured to you, and more will be given to you who hear.

Mark 12, 17 Jesus answered them, "Render unto Caesar the things that are Caesar's, and to God the things that are God's."

Luke 6, 29 To him who strikes you on the cheek, offer also the other: and from him who takes away your cloak, don't withhold your coat also. 30 Give to everyone who asks you, and don't ask him who takes away your goods to give them back again.

Luke 6, 35 But love your enemies, and do good, and lend, expecting nothing back; and your reward will be great, and you will be children of the Most High; . . .

Luke 6, 38 "Give and it will be given unto you: good measure, pressed down, shaken together, and running over, will be given to you. For with the same measure you measure it will be measured back to you.

Luke 11, 41 But give for gifts to the needy those things which are within, and behold, all things will be clean to you.

Luke 12, 33 Sell what you have and give gifts to the needy. Make for yourselves purses which don't grow old, a treasure in the heavens that doesn't fail, where no thief approaches, neither moth destroys.

Luke 14, 12 He also said to the one who had invited him, "When you make a dinner or a supper, don't call your friends, nor your brothers, nor your kinsmen, nor rich neighbors, or perhaps they might also return the favor, and pay you back. 13 But when you make a feast, ask the poor, the maimed, the lame, or the blind; 14 and you will be blessed, because they don't have the resources to repay you. For you will be repaid in the resurrection of the righteous."

Luke 16, 9 I tell you, make for yourselves friends by means of unrighteous mammon, so that when you fail, they may receive you into eternal tents.

God and Money

Matthew 6, 24 "No one can serve two masters, for either he will hate the one and love the other; or else he will be devoted to one and despise the other. You can't serve both God and mammon.

Matthew 22, 19 Show me the tax money." 20 He asked them, "Whose is this image and inscription?" 21 They said to him, "Caesar's." Then he said to them, "Give therefore to Caesar the things that are Caesar's, and to God the things that are God's."

Mark 12, 17 Jesus answered them, "Render to Caesar the things that are Caesar's, and to God the things that are God's."

Luke 16, 13 No servant can serve two masters, for either he will hate the one, and love the other; or else he will hold to one, and despise the other. You aren't able to serve God and Mammon."

Luke 20, 24 Show me a denarius. Whose image and inscription are on it?" They answered. "Caesar's." 25 He said to them, "Then give to Caesar the things that are Caesar's, and to God the things that are God's."

Golden Rule

Matthew 7, 12 Therefore whatever you desire for men to do to you, you shall also do to them; for this is the law and the prophets.

Matthew 19,19 . . . .And, 'You shall love you neighbor as yourself.'"

Matthew 22, 39 . . . 'You shall love your neighbor as yourself.'

Luke 6, 31 "As you would like people to do to you, do exactly so to them.

Greatest and Second Greatest Commandments

Matthew 22, 36 "Teacher, which is the greatest commandment in the law?" 37 Jesus said to him, "'You shall love the Lord your God with all your heart, with all your soul, and with all your mind.' 38 This is the first and great commandment. 39 A second likewise is this, 'You shall love your neighbor as yourself.' 40 The whole law and prophets depend on these two commandments."

Mark 12, 28 . . . "Which commandment is the greatest of all?" 29 Jesus answered, "The greatest is, "Hear, Israel, the Lord our God, the Lord is one: 30 You shall love the Lord your God with all your heart, and with all your soul, and with all your mind, and with all your strength.' This is the first commandment. 31 The second is like this, 'You shall love your neighbor as yourself.' There is no other commandment greater than these.

Greed

Luke 12, 15 He said to them, "Beware, Keep yourselves from covetousness, for a man's life doesn't consist of the abundance of the things which he possesses."

Guidance to the Seventy Apostles for their Travels

Luke 10, 1 Now after these things, the Lord also appointed seventy others, and sent them two by two ahead of him into every city and place where he was about to come. 2 Then he said to them, "The harvest is indeed plentiful, but the laborers are few. Pray therefore to the Lord of the harvest, that he may send out laborers into his harvest. 3 Go your ways. Behold, I send you out as lambs among wolves. 4 Carry no purse, nor wallet, nor sandals. Greet no one on the way. 5 Into whatever house you enter, first say, 'Peace be to this house.' 6 If a son of peace is there, your peace will rest on him; but if not, it will return to you. 7 Remain in that same house, eating and drinking the things they give, for the laborer is worthy of his wages. Don't go from house to house. 8 Into whatever city you enter, and they receive you, eat the things that are set before you. 9 Heal the sick who are there, and tell them, 'God's Kingdom has come near to you.' 10 But into whatever city you enter, and they don't receive you, go out into its streets and say, 11 'Even the dust from your city that clings to us, we wipe off against you. Nevertheless know this, that God's Kingdom has come near to you.'

Luke 10,19 Behold, I give you authority to tread on serpents and scorpions, and over all the power of the enemy. Nothing will in any way hurt you. 20 Nevertheless, don't rejoice in this, that the spirits are subject to you, but rejoice that your names are written in heaven."

Hate

Matthew 18, 10 See that you don't despise one of these little ones, for I tell you that in heaven their angels always see the face of my Father who is in heaven.

Have Patience then Witness

Acts 1, 4 Being assembled together with them, he commanded them, "Don't depart from Jerusalem, but wait for the promise of the Father, which you heard from me. 5 For John indeed baptized with water, but you will be baptized in the Holy Spirit not many days from now." 6 Therefore when they had come together, they asked him, "Lord, are you now restoring the kingdom of Israel?" 7 He said to them, "It isn't for you to know times or seasons which the Father has set within his own authority. 8 But you will receive power when the Holy Spirit has come upon you. You will be witnesses to me in Jerusalem, in all Judea and Samaria, and to the uttermost parts of the earth."

Helping People as Related to the Last Judgment

Matthew 25, 34 Then the King will tell those on his right hand, 'Come, blessed of my Father, inherit the Kingdom prepared for you from the foundation of the world; 35 for I was hungry, and you gave me food to eat. I was thirsty, and you gave me drink. I was a stranger, and you took me in. 36 I was naked, and you clothed me. I was sick, and you visited me. I was in prison, and you came to me. 37 "Then the righteous will answer him saying, 'Lord, when did we see you hungry, and feed you; or thirsty, and give you a drink? 38 When did we see you as a stranger, and take you in; or naked, and clothe you? 39 When did we see you sick, or in prison, and come to you?' 40 "The King will answer them, 'Most certainly I tell you, because you did it to one of the least of these my brothers, you did it to me.'

Holy Eucharist

Matthew 26, 26 As they were eating, Jesus took bread, gave thanks for it, and broke it. He gave to the disciples, and said, "Take, eat, this is my body." 27 He took a cup, gave thanks, and gave to them, saying, "All of you drink it, 28 for this is my blood of the new covenant, which is poured out for many for the remission of sins.

Mark 14, 22 As they were eating, Jesus took bread, and when he had blessed, he broke it, and gave to them, and said, "Take, eat. This is my body." 23 He took the cup, and when he had given thanks, he gave to them. They all drank of it. 24 He said to them, "This is my blood of the new covenant, which is poured out for many.

Luke 22, 17 He received a cup, and when he had given thanks, he said, "Take this, and share it among yourselves, . . . 19 He took bread, and when he had given thanks, he broke, and gave it to them, saying, "This is my body which is given for you. Do this in memory of me." 20 Likewise, he took the cup after supper, saying, "This cup is the new covenant in my blood, which is poured out for you.

Holy Spirit

Matthew 12, 32 Whoever speaks a word against the Son of Man, it will be forgiven him; but whoever speaks against the Holy Spirit, it will not be forgiven him, neither in this age, nor in that which is to come.

Mark 3, 29 but whoever may blaspheme against the Holy Spirit never has forgiveness, but is subject to eternal condemnation."

Mark 13, 11 When they lead you away and deliver you up, don't be anxious beforehand, or premeditate what you will say, but say whatever will be given you in that hour. For it is not you who speak, but the Holy Spirit.

Luke 12, 10 Everyone who speaks a word against the Son of Man will be forgiven, but those who blaspheme against the Holy Spirit will not be forgiven.

John 20, 21 Jesus therefore said to them again, "Peace be to you. As the Father has sent me, even so I send you." 22 When he had said this, he breathed on them, and said to them, "Receive the Holy Spirit!

Humility

Luke 14, 11 For everyone who exalts himself will be humbled, and whoever humbles himself will be exalted."

Luke 17, 10 Even so you also, when you have done all the things that are commanded you, say, 'We are unworthy servants. We have done our duty.'"

Luke 18, 14 . . . for everyone who exalts himself will be humbled, but he who humbles himself will be exalted."

Importance of Keeping Christ's Commandments

John 14, 21 One who has my commandments and keeps them, that person is one who loves me. One who loves me will be loved by my Father, and I will love him, and will reveal myself to him."

Judging

Matthew 7, 1 "Don't judge, so that you won't be judged.

Mark 4, 24 he said to them, "Take heed of what you hear. With whatever measure you measure, it will be measured to you, and more will be given to you who hear.

Mark 8, 32 He spoke to them openly. Peter took him and began to rebuke him. 33 But he, turning around, and seeing his disciples, rebuked Peter, and said, "Get behind me, Satan! For you have in mind not the things of God, but the things of men."

Luke 6, 37 Don't judge, and you won't be judged. . . .

John 7, 24 Don't judge according to appearance, but judge righteous judgment."

Listening/Hearing

Matthew 11,15 He who has ears to hear, let him hear.

Matthew 13, 9 He who has ears to hear, let him hear."

Matthew 13, 43 Then the righteous will shine like the sun in the Kingdom of their Father. He who has ears to hear, let him hear.

Matthew 15, 10 He summoned the multitude, and said to them, "Hear, and understand.

Mark 4, 23 If any man has ears to hear, let him hear." 24 He said to them, "Take heed what you hear. With whatever measure you measure, it will be measured to you, and more will be given to you who hear.

Mark 7, 14 He called all the multitude to himself, and said to them, "Hear me, all of you, and understand. . . . 16 If anyone has ears to hear, let him hear!"

Luke 8, 5 "The farmer went out to sow his seed. As he sowed, some fell along the road and was trampled under foot, ... 8 Other fell into the good ground, and grew, and produced one hundred times as much fruit." As he said these things, he called out, "He who has ears to hear, let him hear!"

Luke 9, 44 "Let these words sink into your ears, for the Son of Man will be delivered up into the hands of men."

Live in Christ

John 15, 4 Remain in me, and I in you. As the branch can't bear fruit by itself unless it remains in the vine, so neither can you, unless you remain in me. 5 I am the vine. You are the branches. He who remains in me and I in him bears much fruit, for apart from me you can do nothing.

Loaning

Matthew 5, 42 Give to him who asks you, and don't turn away him who desires to borrow from you.

Luke 6, 35 But love your enemies, and do good, and lend, expecting nothing back; and your reward will be great, and you will be children of the Most High;

Loving

Matthew 5, 44 But I tell you, love your enemies, bless those who curse you, do good to those who hate you, and pray for those who mistreat you and persecute you.

Matthew 19, 19 . . . . And, 'You shall love your neighbor as yourself.'"

Mark 12, 30 You shall love the Lord your God with all your heart, and with all your soul, and with all your mind, and with all your strength.' 31 The second is like this, 'You shall love your neighbor as yourself. There is no other commandment greater than these."

Luke 6, 27 "But I tell you who hear: love your enemies, do good to those who hate you, . . .

Luke 6, 35 But love your enemies, and do good, . . .

John 13, 34 A new commandment I give to you, that you love one another. Just as I have loved you, you also love one another.

John 14, 21 One who has my commandments and keeps them, that person is one who loves me. One who loves me will be loved by my Father, and I will love him, and will reveal myself to him.

John 15, 9 Even as the Father has loved me, I have loved you. Remain in my love.

John 15, 12 "This is my commandment, that you love one another, even as I have loved you.

John 15, 17 "I command these things to you, that you may love one another.

John 21,15 So when they had eaten their breakfast, Jesus said to Simon Peter, "Simon, son of Jonah, do you love me more than these?" He said to him, "Yes, Lord; you know that I have affection for you." He said to him, "Feed my lambs." 16 He said to him a second time, "Simon, son of Jonah, do you love me?" He said to him, "Yes, Lord; you know that I have affection for you." He said to him, "Tend my sheep." 17 He said to him the third time, "Simon, son of Jonah, do you have affection for me?" Peter was grieved because he asked him the third time, "Do you have affection for me?" He said to him, "Lord, you know everything. You know that I have affection for you." Jesus said to him, "Feed my sheep.

Making Oaths on Things

Matthew 5, 33 "Again you have heard that it was said to the ancient ones, 'You shall not make false vows, but shall perform to the Lord your vows,' 34 but I tell you, don't swear at all: neither by heaven, for it is the throne of God; nor by the earth, for it is the footstool of his feet; nor by Jerusalem, for it is the city of the great King. 36 Neither shall you swear by your head, for you can't make one hair white or black. 37 But let your 'Yes' be 'Yes' and your 'No' be 'No.' Whatever is more than these is of the evil one.

Making Peace

Matthew 18, 15 "If your brother sins against you, go, show him his fault between him and you alone. If he listens to you, you have gained back your brother. 16 But if he doesn't listen, take one or two more with you, that at the mouth of two or three witnesses every word may be established. 17 If he refuses to listen to them, tell it to the assembly. If he refuses to hear the assembly also, let him be to you as a Gentile or a tax collector.

Mercy

Luke 6, 36 "Therefore be merciful, even as your Father is also merciful.

Luke 10, 36 Now which of these three do you think seemed to be a neighbor to him who fell among the robbers?" 37 He said, "He who showed mercy on him." Then Jesus said to him, "Go and do likewise."

Moses' Laws

Matthew 23, 1 Then Jesus spoke to the multitudes and to his disciples, 2 saying "The scribes and the Pharisees sat at Moses' seat. 3 All things therefore whatever they tell you to observe, observe and do, but don't do their works; for they say, and don't do.

Orders to John

Revelation 1, 10 I was in the spirit on the Lord's day, and I heard behind me a loud voice, like a trumpet 11 saying, "What you see, write in a book and send to the seven assemblies: to Ephesus, Smyrna, Pergamum, Thyatira, Sardis, Philadelphia, and to Laodicea." . . . 17 When I saw him, I fell at his feet like a dead man. He laid his right hand on me, saying, "Don't be afraid. I am the first and the last, 18 and the Living one. I was dead, and behold, I am alive forever and ever. Amen. I have the keys of Death and Hades. 19 Write therefore the things which will happen hereafter.

Revelation 2, 1 "To the angel of the assembly in Ephesus write: . . . 7 He who has an ear, let him hear what the Spirit says to the assemblies. 8 "To the angel of the assembly in Smyrna write: . . . 11 He who has an ear, let him hear what the Spirit says to the assemblies. 12 "To the angel of the assembly in Pergamum write: . . . 17 He who has an ear, let him hear what the Spirit says to the assemblies. 18 "To the angel of the assembly in Thyatira write: . . . 29 He who has an ear, let him hear what the Spirit says to the assemblies.

Revelation 3, 1 "And to the angel of the assembly in Sardis write: . . . 6 He who has an ear, let him hear what the Spirit says to the assemblies. 7 "To the angel of the assembly in Philadelphia write: . . . 13 He who has an ear, let him hear what the Spirit says to the assemblies. 14 "To the angel of the assembly in Laodicea write: . . . 22 He who has an ear, let him hear what the Spirit says to the assemblies."

Praying

Matthew 5, 44 But I tell you, love your enemies, bless those who curse you, do good to those who hate you, and pray for those who mistreat and persecute you, . . .

Matthew 6, 5 "When you pray, you shall not be as hypocrites, for they love to stand and pray in the synagogues and in the corners of the streets, that they may be seen by men. Most certainly, I tell you, they have received their reward. 6 But you, when you pray, enter into your inner room, and having shut your door, pray to your Father who is in secret, and your Father who sees in secret will reward you openly. 7 In praying, don't use vain repetitions, as the Gentiles do; for they think that they will be heard for their much speaking. 8 Therefore don't be like them, for your Father knows what things you need, before you ask him. 9 Pray like this: 'Our Father in heaven, may your name be kept holy. 10 Let your Kingdom come. Let your will be done on earth as it is in heaven. 11 Give us today our daily bread. 12 Forgive us our debts, as we also forgive our debtors. 13 Bring us not into temptation, but deliver us from the evil one. For yours is the Kingdom, the power, and the glory forever. Amen.'

Matthew 9, 37 Then he said to his disciples, "The harvest indeed is plentiful, but the laborers are few. 38 Pray therefore that the Lord of the harvest will send out laborers into his harvest."

Matthew 24, 20 Pray that your flight will not be in the winter, nor on a Sabbath, . . .

Matthew 26, 41 Watch and pray, that you don't enter into temptation. The spirit indeed is willing, but the flesh is weak."

Mark 11, 21 Peter, remembering, said to him, "Rabbi, look! The fig tree which you cursed has withered away." 22 Jesus answered them, "Have faith in God. 23 For most certainly I tell you, whoever may tell this mountain, 'Be taken up and cast into the sea,' and doesn't doubt in his heart, but believes that what he says is happening; he shall have whatever he says. 24 Therefore I tell you, all things whatever you pray and ask for, believe that you have received them, and you shall have them. 25 Whenever you stand praying, forgive, if you have anything against anyone; so that your Father, who is in heaven, may also forgive you your transgressions.

Mark 13, 18 Pray that your flight won't be in winter.

Mark 13, 33 Watch, keep alert, and pray; for you don't know when the time is.

Mark 14, 38 Watch and pray, that you may not enter into temptation. The spirit indeed is willing, but the flesh is weak."

Luke 6, 28 bless those who curse you, and pray for those who mistreat you.

Luke 10, 2 Then he said to them, "The harvest is indeed plentiful, but the laborers are few. Pray therefore to the Lord of the harvest, that he may send out laborers into his harvest.

Luke 11, 2 He said to them, "When you pray, say, 'Our Father in heaven, may your name be kept holy. May your Kingdom come. May your will be done on earth, as it is in heaven. 3 Give us day by day our daily bread. 4 Forgive us our sins, for we ourselves also forgive everyone who is indebted to us. Bring us not into temptation, but deliver us from the evil one."

Luke 21, 36 Therefore be watchful all the time, praying that you may be counted worthy to escape all these things that will happen, and to stand before the Son of Man."

Luke 22, 40 When he was at the place, he said to them, "Pray that you don't enter into temptation."

Luke 22, 46 . . . "Why do you sleep? Rise and pray that you may not enter into temptation."

Preparation for the Second Coming

Matthew 24, 42 Watch, therefore, for you don't know in what hour your Lord comes.

Matthew 25, 13 Watch, therefore, for you don't know the day nor the hour in which the Son of Man is coming.

Luke 12, 35 "Let your waist be dressed and your lamps burning.

Luke 12, 40 Therefore be ready also, for the Son of Man is coming in an hour that you don't expect him."

Luke 21, 7 They asked him, "Teacher, so when will these things be? What is the sign that these things are about to happen" 8 He said, "Watch out that you don't get led astray, for many will come in my name, saying, 'I am he,' and, 'The time is at hand.' Therefore don't follow them. 9 When you hear of wars and disturbances, don't be terrified, for these things must happen first, but the end won't come immediately." 10 Then he said to them, "Nation will rise up against nation, kingdom against kingdom. 11 There will be great earthquakes, famines, and plagues in various places. There will be terrors and great signs from heaven. . . . 20 "But when you see Jerusalem surrounded by armies, then know that its desolation is at hand. . . . 25 There will be signs in the sun, moon, and stars; and on earth anxiety of nations, in perplexity for the roaring of the sea and the waves; 26 men fainting for fear, and for expectation of the things which are coming in a cloud with power and great glory. 28 But when these things begin to happen, look up and lift up your heads, because your redemption is near." . . . 31 Even so you also, when you see these things happening, know that God's Kingdom is near. . . . 34 "So be careful, or your hearts will be loaded down with carousing, drunkenness, and cares of this life, and that day will come on you suddenly. . . . 36 Therefore be watchful all the time, praying that you may be counted worthy to escape all these things that will happen, and to stand before the Son of Man."

Pride

Matthew 6, 1 "Be careful that you don't do your charitable giving before men, to be seen by them, or else you have no reward from your Father who is in heaven. 2 Therefore when you do merciful deeds, don't sound a trumpet before yourself, as the hypocrites do in the synagogues and in the streets, that they may get glory from men. Most certainly I tell you, they have received their reward.

Matthew 6, 16 "Moreover when you fast, don't be like the hypocrites, with sad faces. For they disfigure their faces that they may be seen by men to be fasting. Most certainly I tell you, they have received their reward. 17 But you, when you fast, anoint your head, and wash your face; 18 so that you are not seen by men to be fasting, but by your Father who is in secret, and your Father, who sees in secret, will reward you.

Luke 14, 11 For everyone who exalts himself will be humbled, and whoever humbles himself will be exalted.

Providing Fish for the Disciples' Empty Net

John 21, 5 Jesus therefore said to them, "Children, have you anything to eat?" They answered him, "No." 6 He said to them, "Cast the net on the right side of the boat, and you will find some." They cast it therefore, and now they weren't able to draw it in for the multitude of fish.

Public Display of Self

Matthew 5, 16 Even so, let your light shine before men; that they may see your good works, and glorify your Father who is in heaven.

Luke 20, 46 "Beware of those scribes who like to walk in long robes, and love greetings in the marketplaces, the best seats in the synagogues, and the best places at feasts; 47 who devour widows' houses, and for a pretense make long prayers: these will receive greater condemnation."

Readiness

Matthew 24, 42 Watch therefore, for you don't know in what hour your Lord comes.

Matthew 24, 44 Therefore also be ready, for in an hour you don't expect, the Son of Man will come.

Luke 12, 40 Therefore be ready also, for the Son of Man is coming in an hour that you don't expect him."

Mark 13, 32 But of that day or that hour no one knows, not even the angels in heaven, nor the Son, but only the Father.

Mark 13, 37 What I tell you, I tell all: Watch."

Reforming Your Lives, Repenting

Matthew 4, 17 From that time, Jesus began to preach, and to say, "Repent! For the Kingdom of Heaven is at hand."

Mark 1, 14 . . . Jesus came into Galilee, preaching the Good News of God's Kingdom, 15 and saying, "The time is fulfilled, and God's Kingdom is at hand! Repent, and believe in the Good News."

Luke 13, 1 Now there were some present at the same time who told him about the Galileans, whose blood Pilate had mixed with their sacrifices. 2 Jesus answered them, "Do you think that these Galileans were worse sinners than all the other Galileans, because they suffered such things? 3 I tell you, no, but unless you repent, you will all perish in the same way. 4 Or those eighteen, on whom the tower in Siloam fell and killed them; do you think that they were worse offenders than all the men who dwell in Jerusalem? 5 I tell you, but unless you repent, you will perish in the same way."

Luke 24, 46 He said to them, "Thus it is written, and thus it was necessary for the Christ to suffer and to rise from the dead the third day, 47 and that repentance and remission of sins should be preached in his name to all nations, beginning at Jerusalem.

John 5, 14 Afterward Jesus found him in the temple, and said to him, "Behold, you are made well. Sin no more, so that nothing worse happens to you."

Rejoice

Matthew 28, 8 They departed quickly from the tomb with fear and great joy, and ran to bring his disciples word. 9 As they went to tell his disciples, Jesus met them saying, "Rejoice!" They came and took hold of his feet and worshipped him.

Remember

Luke 24, 44 He said to them, "This is what I told you, while I was still with you, that all things which are written in the law of Moses, the prophets, and the psalms, concerning me must be fulfilled." 45 Then he opened their minds, that they might understand the Scriptures. 46 He said to them, "Thus it is written, and thus it was necessary for the Christ to suffer and to rise from the dead on the third day,

Revelation 22, 7 "Behold, I come quickly. Blessed is he who keeps the words of the prophecy of this book."

Revelation 22, 12 "Behold, I come quickly. My reward is with me, to repay each man according to his work.

Resurrecting Others

Luke 8, 53 They were ridiculing him, knowing that she was dead. 54 But he put them all outside, and taking her by the hand, he called, saying, "Child, arise!" 55 Her spirit returned, and she rose up immediately.

John 11, 43 When he had said this, he cried with a loud voice, "Lazarus, come out!" 44 He who was dead came out, bound hand and foot with wrappings, and his face was wrapped around with a cloth, Jesus said to them, "Free him, and let him go."

Revenge

Matthew 5, 38 "You have heard that it was said, 'An eye for an eye, and a tooth for a tooth.' 39 But I tell you, don't resist him who is evil; but whoever strikes you on your right cheek, turn to him the other also. 40 If anyone sues you to take away your coat, let him have your cloak also. 41 Whoever compels you to go one mile, go with him two.

Luke 6, 29 To him who strikes you on the cheek, offer also the other; and from him who takes away your cloak, don't withhold your coat also. 30 . . . and don't ask him who takes away your goods to give them back again.

Saving

Matthew 6, 19 "Don't lay up treasures for yourselves on earth, where moth and rust consume, and where thieves break through and steal; 20 but lay up for yourselves treasures in heaven, where neither moth nor rust consume, and where thieves don't break through and steal;

Seeing

Mark 3, 32 A multitude was sitting around him, and they told him, "Behold, your mother, your brothers, and your sisters are outside looking for you." 33 He answered them, "Who are my mother and my brothers?" 34 Looking around at those who sat around him, he said, "Behold, my mother and my brothers! 35 For whoever does the will of God is my brother, my sister, and mother."

Mark 13, 23 But you watch. "Behold, I have told you all things beforehand.

Mark 14, 38 Watch and pray, that you might not enter into temptation. The spirit is indeed willing, but the flesh is weak."

Revelation 22, 12 "Behold, I come quickly.

Seek God

Matthew 6, 33 But seek first God's Kingdom, and his righteousness; and all these things will be given to you as well.

Luke 12, 31 But seek God's kingdom, and all these things will be added to you.

Set Free

Luke 6, 37 . . . . Set free and you will be set free.

Speaking during Adversity

Matthew 10, 18 Yes, you will be brought before governors and kings for my sake, for a testimony to them and to the nations. 19 But when they deliver you up, don't be anxious how or what you will say. 20 For it is not you who speak, but the Spirit of your Father who speaks in you.

Luke 12, 11 When they bring you before the synagogues, the rulers, and the authorities, don't be anxious how or what you will answer, or what you will say; 12 for the Holy Spirit will teach you in that same hour what you must say."

Sinning

Mark 9, 42 Whoever will cause one of these little ones who believe in me to stumble, it would be better for him if he were thrown into the sea with a millstone hung around his neck.

John 5, 14 Afterward Jesus found him in the temple, and said to him, "Behold, you are made well. Sin no more, so that nothing worse happens to you."

Taking Care

Matthew 24, 4 Jesus answered them, "Be careful that no one leads you astray.

Mark 13, 5 Jesus, answering, began to tell them, "Be careful that no one leads you astray.

Luke 17, 3 Be careful. If your brother sins against you, rebuke him. If he repents, forgive him.

Luke 21, 34 "So be careful, or your hearts will be loaded down with carousing, drunkenness, and cares of this life, and that day will come on you suddenly.

Teaching

Matthew 7, 6 "Don't give that which is holy to dogs, neither throw your pearls before the pigs, lest perhaps they trample them under their feet, and turn and tear you to pieces.

Matthew 28, 19 Go and make disciples of all nations, . . . 20 teaching them to observe all things that I commanded you.

Testing God

Matthew 4, 7 Jesus said to him, "Again, it is written, 'You shall not test the Lord, your God.'"

Luke 4, 12 Jesus answering, said to him, "It has been said, 'You shall not tempt the Lord you God.'"

The Ascension

John 20, 17 Jesus said to her, "Don't hold me, for I haven't yet ascended to my Father; but go to my brothers and tell them, 'I am ascending to my Father and your Father, to my God and your God."

The Call of Saul (Name Later Changed to Paul)

Acts 9, 4 He fell on the earth, and heard a voice saying to him, "Saul, Saul, why do you persecute me?" 5 He said, "Who are you, Lord?" The Lord said, "I am Jesus, whom you are persecuting. 6 But rise up and enter into the city, then you will be told what you must do."

Acts 9, 10 Now there was a certain disciple at Damascus named Ananias. The Lord said to him in a vision, "Ananias!" He said, "Behold, it's me, Lord." 11 The Lord said to him, "Arise, and go to the street which is called Straight, and inquire in the house of Judah for one named Saul, a man of Tarsus. For behold, he is praying, 12 and in a vision he has seen a man named Ananias coming in and laying his hands on him, that he might receive his sight." . . . 15 But the Lord said to him, "Go your way, for he is my chosen vessel to bear my name before the nations and kings, and the children of Israel.

Acts 22, 7 I fell to the ground, and heard a voice saying to me, 'Saul, Saul, why are you persecuting me?' 8 I answered, 'Who are you, Lord?' He said to me, 'I am Jesus of Nazareth, whom you persecute.' 9 "Those who were with me indeed saw the light and were afraid, but they didn't understand the voice of him who spoke to me. 10 I said, 'What shall I do, Lord?' The Lord said to me, 'Arise, and go into Damascus. There you will be told about all the things which are appointed for you to do.' 11 When I couldn't see for the glory of the light, being led by the hand of those who were with me, I came into Damascus. 12 One Ananias, a devout man according to the law, well reported of by all the Jews who lived in Damascus, 13 came to me, and standing by me said to me, 'Brother Saul, receive your sight!" In that very hour I looked up at him. 14 He said, 'The God of our fathers has appointed you to know his will, and to see the Righteous One, and to hear a voice from his mouth. 15 For you will be a witness for him to all men of what you have seen and heard. 16 Now why do you wait? Arise, be baptized, and wash away your sins, calling on the name of the Lord.' 17 "When I had returned to Jerusalem, and while I prayed in the temple, I fell into a trance, 18 and saw him saying to me, 'Hurry and get out of Jerusalem quickly, because they will not receive testimony concerning me from you.' 19 I said, 'Lord, they themselves know that I imprisoned and beat in every synagogue those who believed in you. 20 When the blood of Stephen, your witness, was shed, I also was standing by, consenting to his death, and guarding the cloaks of those who killed him.' 21 "He said to me, 'Depart, for I will send you out far from here to the Gentiles.'"

Acts 23, 11 The following night, the Lord stood by him and said, "Cheer up, Paul, for as you have testified about me in Jerusalem, so you must testify also at Rome."

Acts 26, 14 When we had all fallen to the earth, I heard a voice saying to me in the Hebrew language, 'Saul, Saul, why are you persecuting me? It is hard for you to kick against the goads.' 15 "I said, 'Who are you, Lord?' "He said, 'I am Jesus, whom you are persecuting. 16 But arise, and stand on your feet, for I have appeared to you for this purpose: to appoint you a servant and a witness both of the things which you have seen, and of the things which I will reveal to you; 17 delivering you from the people, and from the Gentiles, to whom I send you, 18 to open their eyes, that they may turn from darkness to light and from the power of Satan to God, that they may receive remission of sins and an inheritance among those who are sanctified by faith in me.'

The Second Coming

Revelation 22, 12 "Behold I come quickly. My reward is with me, to repay each man according to his work. 13 I am the Alpha and the Omega, the First and the Last, the Beginning and the End. 14 Blessed are those who do his commandments, that they may have the right to the tree of life, and may enter in by the gates into the city. 15 Outside are the dogs, the sorcerers, the sexually immoral, the murderers, the idolaters, and everyone who loves and practices falsehood. 16 I, Jesus, have sent my angel to testify these things to you for the assemblies. I am the root and the offspring of David, the Bright and Morning Star."

The Work of God and Faith in Jesus

John 6, 29 Jesus answered them, "This is the work of God, that you believe in him whom he has sent."

Titles

Matthew 23, 8 But don't you be called 'Rabbi,' for one is your teacher, the Christ, and all of you are brothers. 9 Call no man on earth your father, for one is your Father, he who is in heaven. 10 Neither be called masters, for one is your master, the Christ.

Treating Deficiencies in Others

Luke 6, 42 Or how can you tell your brother, 'Brother, let me remove the speck of chaff that is in your eye,' when you yourself don't see the beam that is in your own eye? You hypocrite! First remove the beam from your own eye, and then you can see

ROLLAND E. STROUP, JR

clearly to remove the speck of chaff that is in your brother's eye.

Luke 17, 3 Be careful. If your brother sins against you, rebuke him. If he repents, forgive him.

Treatment of Adversaries

Luke 6, 27 "But I tell you who hear: love your enemies, do good to those who hate you, 28 bless those who curse you, and pray for those who mistreat you. 29 To him who strikes you on the cheek, offer also the other; and from him who takes away your cloak, don't withhold your coat also.

Luke 12, 58 For when you are going with your adversary before the magistrate, try diligently on the way to be released from him, lest perhaps he drag you to the judge, and the judge deliver you to the officer, and the officer throw you into prison.

Warning

Luke 12, 15 He said to them, "Beware! Keep yourselves from covetousness, for a man's life doesn't consist of the abundance of the things which he possesses."

Wash Each Other's Feet

John 13, 14 If I then, the Lord and Teacher, have washed your feet, you also ought to wash one another's feet. 15 For I have given you an example, that you also should do as I have done to you.

Watch for Signs and be Ready

Matthew 24, 42 Watch therefore, for you don't know in what hour your Lord comes. . . . 44 Therefore also be ready, for in an hour that you don't expect, the Son of Man will come.

Matthew 25, 13 Watch therefore, for you don't know the day nor the hour in which the Son of Man is coming.

Mark 13, 28 "Now from the fig tree learn this parable. When the branch has now become tender, and produces its leaves, you know that the summer is near; 29 even so you also, when you see these things coming to pass, know that it is near, at the doors. . . . 32 But of the day or that hour no one knows, not even the angels in heaven, nor the Son, but only the Father. 33 Watch, keep alert, and pray;

for you don't know when the time is. . . . 37 What I tell you, I tell all: Watch."

Luke 12, 40 Therefore be ready also, for the Son of Man is coming in an hour that you don't expect him."

Weapons

Matthew 26, 52 Then Jesus said to him, "Put your sword back into its place, for all those who take the sword will die by the sword.

John 18, 11 Jesus therefore said to Peter, "Put the sword into its sheath. The cup which the Father has given me, shall I not surely drink it?"

Weeping

Luke 8, 52 All were weeping and mourning her, but he said, "Don't weep. She isn't dead, but sleeping."

Luke 23, 28 But Jesus, turning to them, said, "Daughters of Jerusalem, don't weep for me, but weep for yourselves and for your children.

Work for Christ and God

Luke 9, 49 John answered, "Master, we saw someone casting out demons in your name, and we forbade him, because he doesn't follow with us." 50 Jesus said to him, "Don't forbid him, for he who is not against us is for us."

John 6, 27 Don't work for the food that perishes, but for the food which remains to eternal life, which the Son of Man will give you. For God the Father has sealed him." 28 They said therefore to him, "What must we do, that we may work the works of God?" 29 Jesus answered them, "This is the work of God, that you believe in him whom he has sent."

Worrying

Mathew 6, 25 Therefore I tell you, don't be anxious for your life: what you will eat, or what you will drink; nor yet for your body, what you will wear. Isn't life more than food, and the body more than clothing? . . . . 31 "Therefore don't be anxious, saying, 'What will we eat?', 'What will we drink?' or, 'With what will we be clothed?' . . . 33 But seek first God's Kingdom, and his righteousness; and all these things will be given to you as well.

34 Therefore don't be anxious for tomorrow, for tomorrow will be anxious for itself. Each day's own evil is sufficient.

Mark 6, 48 Seeing them distressed in rowing, for the wind was contrary to them, about the fourth watch of the night he came by, 49 but, when they saw him walking on the sea, supposed that it was a ghost, and cried out; 50 for they all saw him, and were troubled. But he immediately spoke with them, and said to them, "Cheer up! It is I! Don't be afraid."

Mark 13, 11 When they lead you away and deliver you up, don't be anxious beforehand, or premeditate what you will say, but say whatever will be given you in that hour. For it is not you who speak, but the Holy Spirit.

Luke 8, 46 But Jesus said, "Someone did touch me, for I perceived that power has gone out of me." 47 When the woman saw that she was not hidden, she came trembling, and falling down before him declared to him in the presence of the people the reason why she had touched him, and how she was healed immediately. 48 He said to her, "Daughter, cheer up. Your faith has made you well. Go in peace."

Luke 12, 22 He said to his disciples, "Therefore I tell you, don't be anxious for your life, what you will eat, nor yet for your body, what you will wear. . . . 29 Don't seek what you will eat or what you will drink; neither be anxious. . . . 31 But seek God's Kingdom, and all these things will be added to you.

John 14, 27 Peace I Ieave with you. My peace I give to you; not as the world gives, I give to you. Don't let your heart be troubled, neither let it be fearful.

Worshipping

Matthew 4, 10 Then Jesus said to him, "Get behind me, Satan! For it is written, 'You shall worship the Lord your God, and you shall serve him only.'"

Matthew 5, 23 "If therefore you are offering your gift at the altar, and there remember that your brother has anything against you, 24 leave your gift there before the altar, and go your way. First be reconciled to your brother, and then come and offer your gift.

Luke 4, 8 Jesus answered him, "Get behind me Satan! For it is written, 'You shall worship the Lord your God, and you shall serve him only.'"

John 4, 21 Jesus said to her, "Woman, believe me, the hour comes, and now is, when neither in this mountain, nor in Jerusalem, will you worship the Father. 22 You worship that which you don't know. We worship that which we know; for salvation is from the Jews. 23 But the hour comes, and now is, when the true worshippers will worship the Father in spirit and truth, for the Father seeks such to be his worshippers. 24 God is spirit, and those who worship him must worship in spirit and truth.

Printed in the United States
by Baker & Taylor Publisher Services